Aimee and the Tablet

Written by Tom Pinfield

Illustrated by Elisa Rocchi

Collins

Mum looks on the tablet.

Aimee sits with her.

Aimee has a turn.

A box appears.

Aimee has a think.

9

Aimee needs to check with Mum.

11

It is all better now.

13

Aimee and the tablet

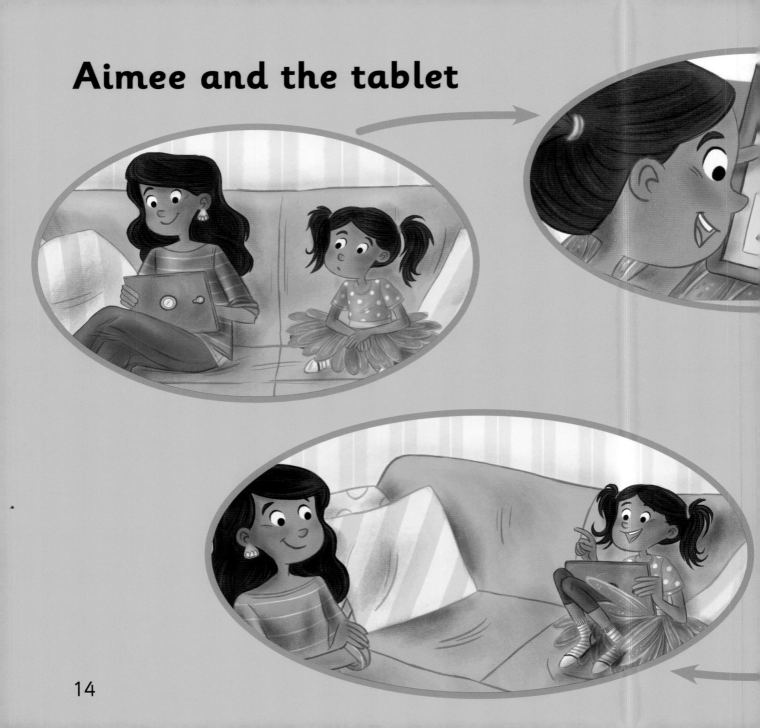

🐾 Review: After reading 🐾

Use your assessment from hearing the children read to choose any GPCs, words or tricky words that need additional practice.

Read 1: Decoding

- Remind the children that two letters together can make just one sound. Ask the children to sound out, then blend these words:

  n/ow   l/oo/k/s   t/ur/n/   g/oa/t   Ai/m/ee

- Remind the children that sometimes three letters can together make just one sound. Ask them to sound out, then blend these words:

  r/igh/t   a/pp/ear/s

Read 2: Prosody

- Model reading each page with expression to the children. After you have read each page, ask the children to have a go at reading with expression.
- On page 5 show children how you invent a voice for Aimee for the speech bubbles.

Read 3: Comprehension

- For every question ask the children how they know the answer. Ask:
  - What is Mum doing at the start of the book? (*looking at her tablet*)
  - What happens when Aimee has a go on the tablet? (*a box appears and it doesn't look right*)
  - What does Aimee decide to do? (*ask her mum for help*)
- Discuss with the children what they would do if they were using a tablet or computer and something unusual or worrying happened. Ask them why it is best to ask an adult for help.